QUILT AS YOU GO FOR BEGINNERS

Simple Guide for Beginners to Learning Quilt As You Go

Copyright@2023

Liza Fineman

Table of Contents

- CHAPTER ONE 3
  - AN EXPLANATION OF THE QUILT-AS-YOU-GO 3
- CHAPTER TWO 8
  - ESSENTIAL TOOLS AND MATERIALS FOR QUILTING 8
- CHAPTER 3 23
  - INSTRUCTIONS FOR MAKING THE QUILT-AS-YOU-GO BLOCK PATTERN 23
- CHAPTER 5 46
  - HOW TO BIND A QUILT 46

CHAPTER ONE

AN EXPLANATION OF THE QUILT-AS-YOU-GO

A quilt is a multi-layered piece of fabric, and it is generally made up of two or more layers of different kinds of fiber or cloth. In most cases, there will be three layers, along with a filler material. These layers customarily consist of a top made of woven fabric, a layer of batting, and a back made of woven fabric, all of which are sewn together using quilting techniques. This technique involves stitching on the face of the fabric, as opposed to only the edges, in order to join the three layers of the cloth together and make it more durable. Patterns created by stitching can be used as a decorative element. The technique known as **"Quilt As You Go"** was developed recently as a quick method for making quilts.

The process of producing a quilt sandwich using completed quilt blocks or rows, batting that has been trimmed to the desired size, and backing, and then quilting the completed block is referred to as **"Quilting As You Go"**. The blocks are then put together on the quilt top, and the back seams are finished by hand. By the time you are finished with the project, you will have a quilt top that has already been quilted. There are many different ways to complete the Quilt As You Go technique, but in the end, you will always end up with a quilted top. Some methods involve sewing the backing onto the quilt as you go along the process of making it, while others involve sewing the backing onto the quilt after it has been completed. Putting the finishing touches on a quilt using the Quilt As You Go method is a quick and simple process that may be done in a variety of different ways.

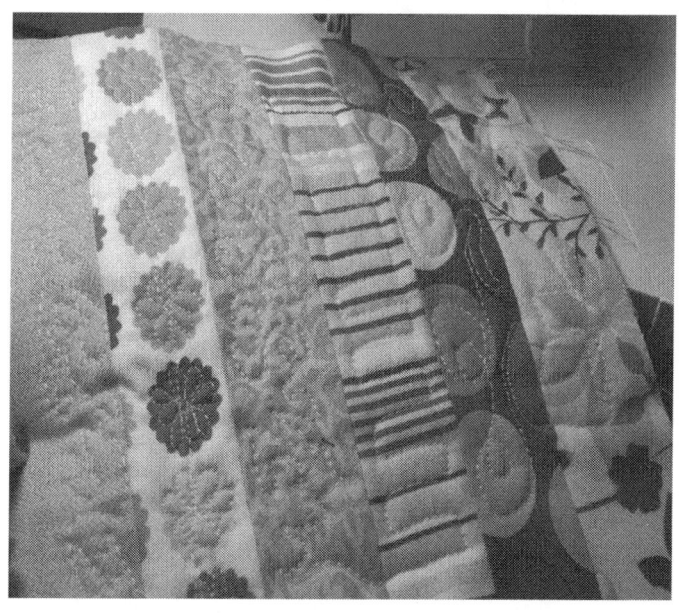

Uses

There are a lot of different customs that surround the many uses of quilt as you go. Important life milestones, such as graduations, weddings, the arrival of a new child, or the departure of a member of the family, may be cause for the creation or gifting of this item.

Advantages of Using the Quilt-As-You-Go Method

1. The Quilt as You Go method is a speedy approach to creating quilts. A reversible project is one in which sides, front and rear, have the potential to be intriguing.

2. If you wish to quilt your quilt using a machine but the throat of your machine is not big enough to accommodate the size of the quilt you are producing, you can still use this approach successfully.

CHAPTER TWO

ESSENTIAL TOOLS AND MATERIALS FOR QUILTING

When learning a new trade, it is only natural to need a few different kinds of tools. Quilting is similar to other crafts in that it requires certain tools and supplies to ensure accurate cutting and straightforward sewing. This guide to Quilting Supplies will help you determine the suitable tools with which to start your stitching adventure so that you can get started quilting.

Sewing Machine

It is not necessary for a reliable sewing machine to be an expensive one, and all it actually needs to be able to do is sew in a straight line consistently.

It is imperative that you remember to bring the needles for the sewing machine. For the vast majority of projects, a Universal 80/12 needle is all that is required. Always start with a fresh needle to guarantee uniform stitches. If you start to observe stitches being skipped, it is time to switch to a different pair of needles.

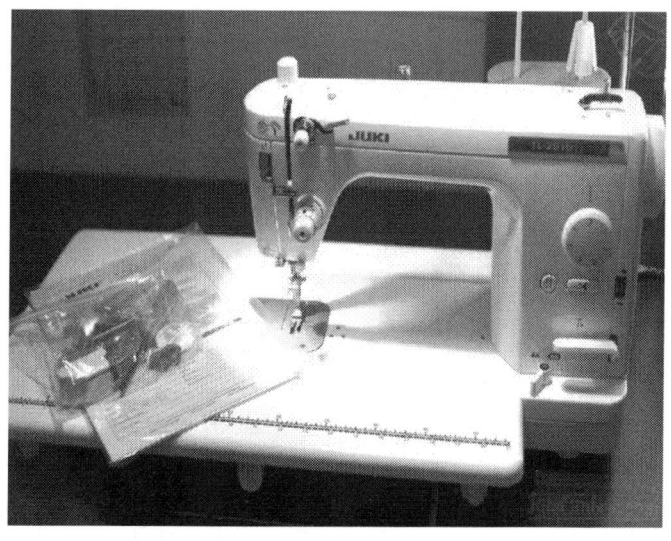

Rotary cutter

Quilting requires careful cutting, and the only way to achieve this level of accuracy is to become proficient in the use of a rotary cutter and a mat that can mend itself. Accurate cutting results in exact piecing. You will be able to move on to more rapid piecing techniques like as chain piecing if you have mastered this talent and are confident in your abilities.

This one-of-a-kind tool features blades that are extremely sharp and is available in a range of different sizes. Therefore it is recommended that you go to a local quilt shop where you may try out many different rotary cutters to determine which one fits your hand the most comfortably.

Self-Healing Cutting Mat

To safeguard your cutting surface and ensure that the rotary blade stays as sharp as possible, you absolutely need to invest in a cutting mat that can repair itself. If you have the room, I would recommend investing in a cutting mat that is 24 inches by 36 inches. Not only does it offer enough surface area to suit a variety of different crafts, but it also fits on top of most tables.

Remember that cutting mats need to be stored in a flat position. If you are limited on room, you might want to look into purchasing a cutting mat that is 18 inches by 24 inches or one that folds up.

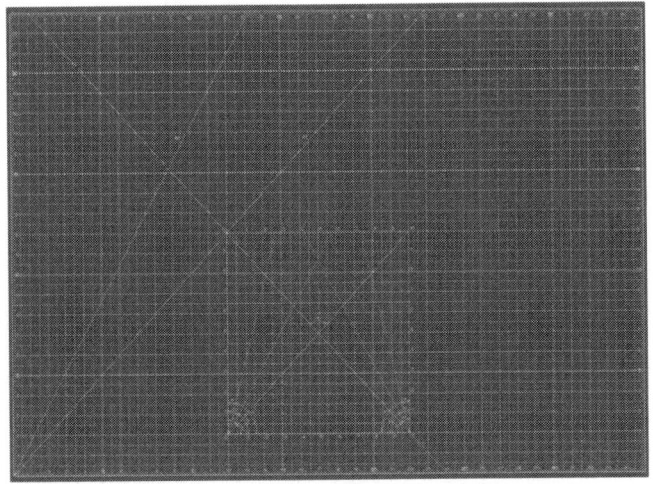

Acrylic Quilting Ruler

Another essential item for the cutting process is a quilting ruler. When using a rotary cutter, you won't have to worry about these rulers slipping because they are see-through and feature a surface that provides a good grip. The majority of them have quilting-specific markers, which make it easier to make precise cuts.

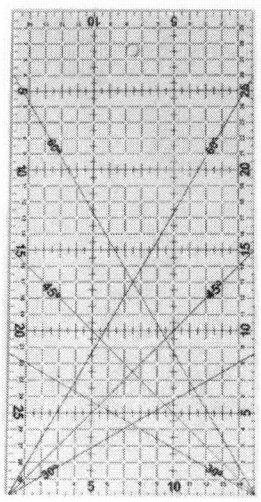

Iron

You do not need to spend a lot of money on an iron because all you need is one that can get hot very quickly and has a steam feature.

Construct an ironing board that is robust enough to take care of your quilt once all of the individual pieces have been added. It's possible that you already have an iron and a board to use with it, and that will do just well. If you put them in a neat stack next to your sewing machine, you will have the perfect environment for quilting.

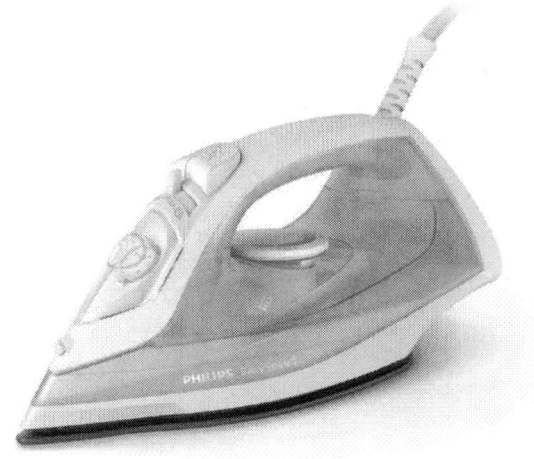

The Needle and the Thread

Your quilt is only as durable as the thread that is used to connect each individual square. The best weight for use, 50wt, and an excellent quality thread made of 100 percent cotton all by itself. Because the thread is so fine, it does not create too much bulk, so this is an extremely important consideration during the piecing process.

Fabric

If you want to make a quilt, you are going to need some fabric. Make sure that the cotton fabric you use for your projects is of a good quality and is made specifically for quilting.

The materials that were used do make a difference in terms of quality. Cotton that is of a higher quality starts with a better product and has a lower risk of bleeding while it is being washed.

When you first begin started, it goes without saying that you should select the materials that are of the finest possible quality that are still within your price range.

Batting

Insulation is provided by the material known as **"batting,"** which is sewn between the quilt's top and back layers. This is the middle layer of your "quilt sandwich," and in addition to providing additional warmth to the quilt, it also helps to puff up the design of the stitching. There are several different kinds of batting, each of which comes in a variety of fiber contents, lofts (the thickness of the batting), and sizes. Wool, silk, bamboo, and blends of cotton and polyester are suitable alternatives to cotton and polyester when it comes to quilt batting. Cotton and polyester are the most common forms of batting used.

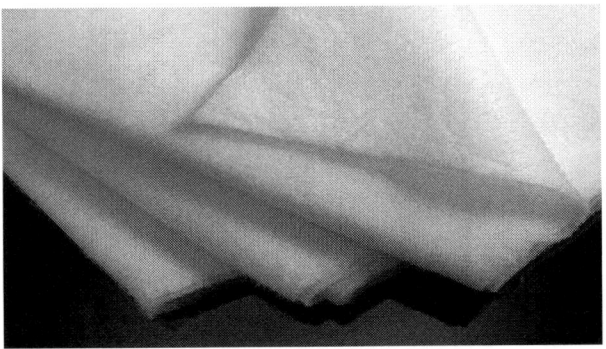

Fabric Scissors

The usage of a pair of sewing scissors is required in order to complete any kind of stitching. In quilting, scissors are used mostly for snipping and clipping very small pieces of fabric.

Pins

Due to the fact that you will most likely be pinning through three layers, you should make sure that your pins are at least 1.5 to 2 inches long.

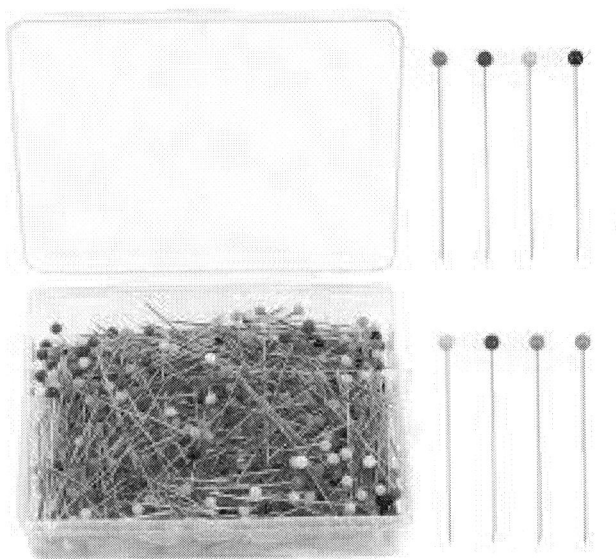

Fabric Marker

Marker that can be removed with water is best to use. The fact that any markings may be erased with a light mist of water is one of the reasons why using fabric pen is preferable.

CHAPTER 3

INSTRUCTIONS FOR MAKING THE QUILT-AS-YOU-GO BLOCK PATTERN

The art of quilting is undeniably satisfying, and the Quilt-As-You-Go concept elevates quilting to a whole new level of coolness.

The fundamental concept here is to quilt all of your layers together as you are piecing your quilt together. This will allow you to work with pieces that are smaller and easier to manage. You can accomplish this in a variety of different ways, but the fundamental concept remains the same: you begin by stacking your pieced blocks, followed by batting and backing that are both cut to the same size, sandwiching these three layers together, and then quilting them before you actually join the blocks together.

Supplies Needed

For Quilt as You Go, you will require the following items:

1. Sewing Machine

2. Sewing Supplies

3. Rotary Cutter

4. Ruler

5. Self Healing Mat

6. Scissors

7. Fabric

8. Batting

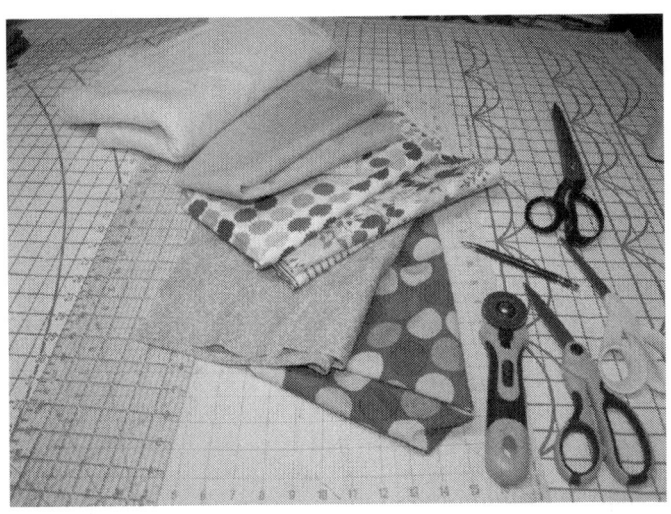

Step 1

Make your Plan

The first thing you should do is draw up a plan. Determine the size of the finished project you want it to be as well as the design you want it to have, and then calculate the amount of yardage you will need to achieve that size. This would go pretty much the same way as your regular quilt project, the only difference being that your backing will all be pieced, so it won't be necessary to have straight yardage for your backing. Which will allows you to make use of the scraps!

Step 2

Determine the Dimensions of Your Blocks, Batting, and Back.

1. I've decided to make a quilt for a baby, which will be approximately 36 inches by 45 inches when it's finished.

2. The layout called for four blocks to be placed across and five to be placed down, and each completed block measured 9 inches. This is only for the purpose of the instructional guide; however, you are free to experiment with a variety of sizes and patterns as you work on your project.

3. After you have finished trimming the top blocks, you will then need to trim the backing squares so that they are exactly the same size as the top blocks.

Top Block

Backing Block

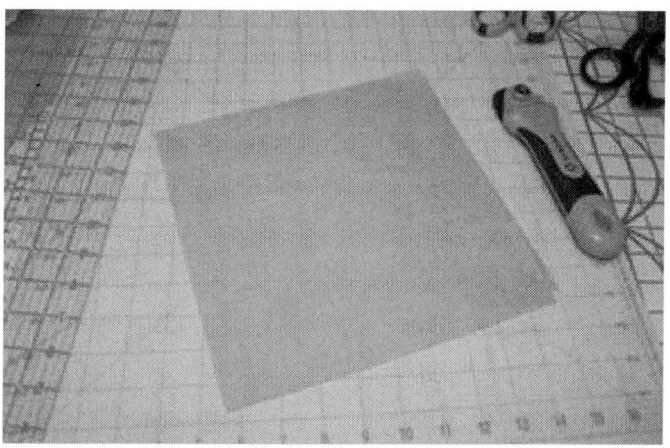

4. Once you have the top and the backing cut to size, proceed to cut the batting to the appropriate dimensions. This part of the process is a little bit different because the seam allowance on your batting should not have any at all.

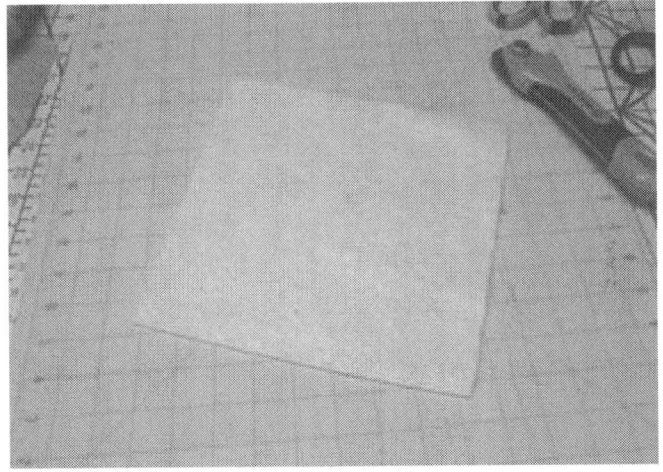

Note that if you let the batting run into the seam, you will end up with far too much bulk in the seams of your project. For instance, I made sure that each of the batting squares in my quilt had an even 9 inches.

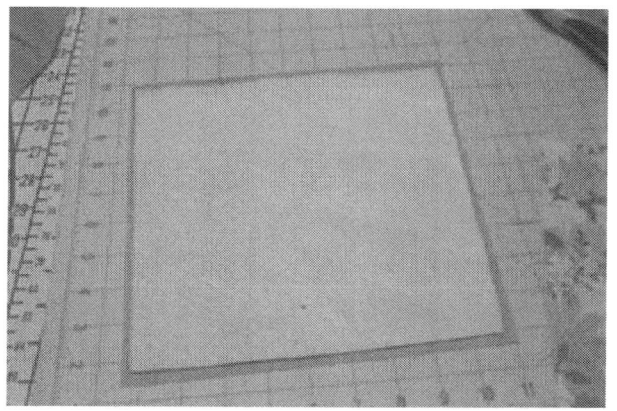

Note

After I was done piecing my top blocks together, I trimmed them down to be 9 inches plus a seam allowance of 1/4 inch. However, I strongly advise utilizing a border of at least half an inch (1/2inch) on each side of each block.

Step 3

Assemble some Fabric Sandwiches

After you have completed piecing all of your blocks and have trimmed them to the appropriate size, you will need to stack your sandwiches.

1. Before you can begin to stack them, you will need to begin by placing your backing fabric, with the wrong side facing up, on your work surface.

2. Arrange your batting squares in a square pattern on top of this. Be sure to position it in the middle, leaving an

equal amount of seam allowance all the way around each side.

3. After you have positioned your batting, place your top block on top of it with the correct side facing up. Make sure that it is carefully aligned with the backing square that is below it.

4. After you have arranged all of your layers as you desire, the next step is to baste them. You can simply pin them, like I have done, or spray baste them... whatever method you choose, as long as it gets the job done.

Step 4

Quilt!

When you have finished basting all of your layers, the next step is to quilt your blocks.

The manner in which you choose to quilt your blocks is completely up to your discretion. Quilting it can be done in either straight lines or free-form shapes... In essence, you should act in a manner that is most natural to you.

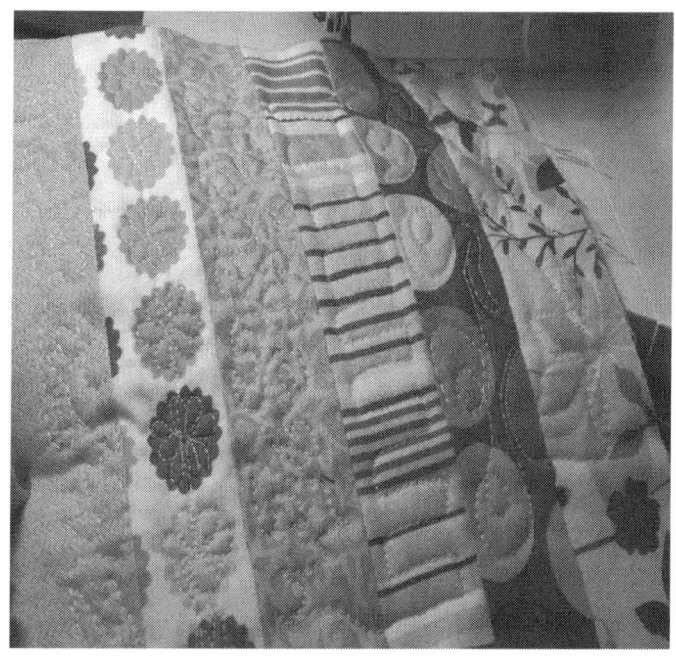

Note

Remembering to avoid sewing into your seam allowance is the single most important thing to keep in mind. If you sew into the seam allowance, it will be a major pain in the rear when you get to the later steps of the process. Therefore, it is not a bad idea to take a marking pencil that can be easily removed and mark around the edges so that you know where to stop when you are finished.

Step 5

Joining Your Blocks

When you have a sizable pile of finished quilt blocks, you can finally begin piecing them together into the final product.

In order to join squares, place two blocks so that their right sides are touching. Pin just the top layers carefully to keep them together. You want to avoid stitching through the backing fabric at all costs. When I was stitching the tops together, I found that it was easiest to either pin or press the backing out of the way while I worked.

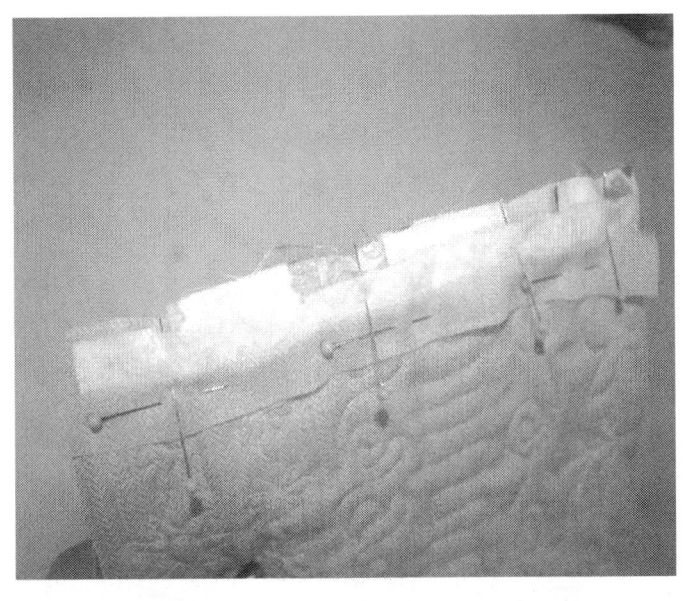

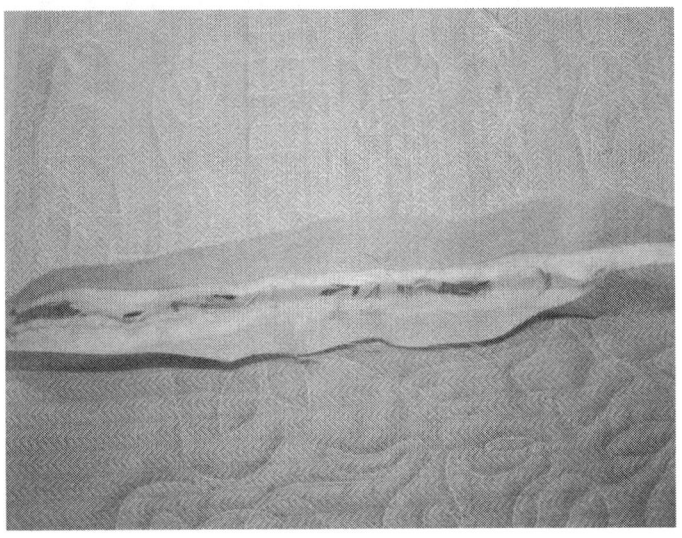

Step 6

Press your Seam

1. After you have successfully joined the two blocks together just at the top layer, press the seam.

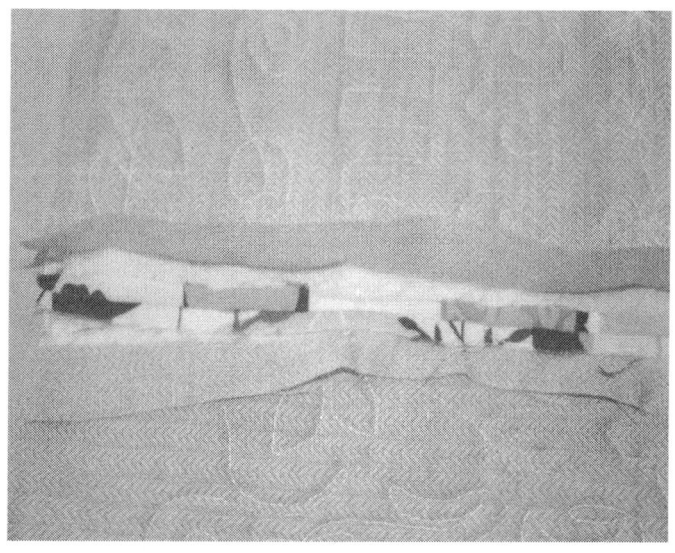

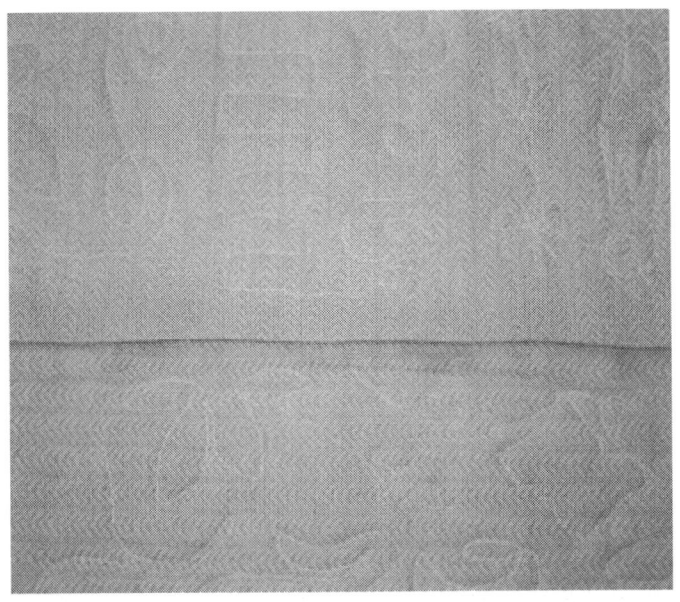

2. Next, smooth the backing fabric back over the back of the seam, and then fold over and pin one edge.

Step 7

Complete the Back Seams

After all of the stitches in a row have been joined together, you should reverse your work and finish the back seams.

You could either choose to stitch it by hand like I have done or you could carefully line up your backing and pin it before using a machine to stitch it all down. I stitched as neatly and inconspicuously as I could, and it was easier for me to do it that way.

When you are stitching your back, you should make sure that you do not leave any of your seams open on the top or bottom. This will ensure that when you join your rows together, you will be able to open your layers in a manner that is horizontally aligned.

Step 8

Join your Rows

After you have completed stitching each row, you can then join the rows together using the same methods that you applied when you were assembling the rows from the individual blocks.

In addition, once you have completed the back of each row, you should also complete the seams that will be used to join the rows together.

Step 9

Finish It up

After you have completed the piecing of your quilt, you will bind it in the same manner as you would a traditional quilt. Check out the following chapter for the complete instructions on how to bind your quilt.

CHAPTER 5

HOW TO BIND A QUILT

The process of covering the unfinished edges of a quilt with strips of fabric is referred to as quilt binding. It is the last step in the process of making a quilt, and it prevents the raw edges from coming apart or fraying. Even though the majority of quilters believe that the binding phase is the most time-consuming part of the process, this is not always the case if you use your sewing machine to do it. This is a common method of finishing a quilt because it saves time (when compared to hand sewing) and it completes the quilt by providing a border edge that is perfectly finished.

The binding is produced by sewing together a number of narrow strips of fabric to create a single long strip that is approximately a little bit longer than the perimeter of the quilt (or outside edge). Whenever we extend the length of the binding strip, we usually add between 5 and 15 inches. In order to ensure that it complements properly and adds an attractive finishing touch to the quilt, it is frequently made out of the same fabric as the top of the quilt. This is done in order to ensure that the quilt is properly bound.

The Binding Can Be Folded in a Number of Different Ways

There are two ways to fold the quilt binding, which are referred to as double fold binding and single fold binding respectively.

Binding with a Double Fold

The double-fold method is the method of quilt binding that is used the most frequently. This pretty much indicates that the binding strip needs to be folded in half before it can be attached to the quilt. Because it produces a binding that is both more robust and long-lasting, this technique is the one that should be used.

Binding with a Single Fold Pattern

Before sewing the fabric strip onto the quilt, the single-fold binding method requires that you let the strip of fabric unfold so that it can be seen more clearly. The fact that your strips are shorter gives you the primary benefit of using less fabric when you employ this method; however, in comparison to the double strip method, this one is not as reliable. Utilize this method when stitching onto quilts that will not receive a significant amount of wear and tear, such as an art quilt or an ornamental piece.

Note

1. When I'm cutting fabric, I almost always do it crosswise because it's the quickest, easiest, and most efficient way to do it.

2. If you are just starting out with quilt binding, the two widths that are most commonly used are 2 ¼" and 2 ½". (using the double-fold method and a quarter-inch seam). However, you can choose to use a different seam allowance and cut the binding to a width that is either smaller or larger depending on the aesthetic that you are going for and the type of binding that you select. For instance, if you want a wide binding, cut the strips to

a width of three inches and use a seam allowance of three quarters of an inch.

3. The width of the binding strips is typically 2 ¼" and a quarter of an inch (1/4inch) is allowed for seam allowance when sewing them to the quilt.

The Process of Making Binding

Because it is more long-lasting, continuous, has mitered corners, and is finished with hand stitching, the double fold approach is the method that I prefer to use when binding my quilts.

Step 1

To get started, take your rotary cutter and quilting ruler and trim away any excess backing and batting from around the border (edge) of your quilt. Align the ruler with the unfinished edge of the top of the quilt, and then cut away any excess batting and backing fabric.

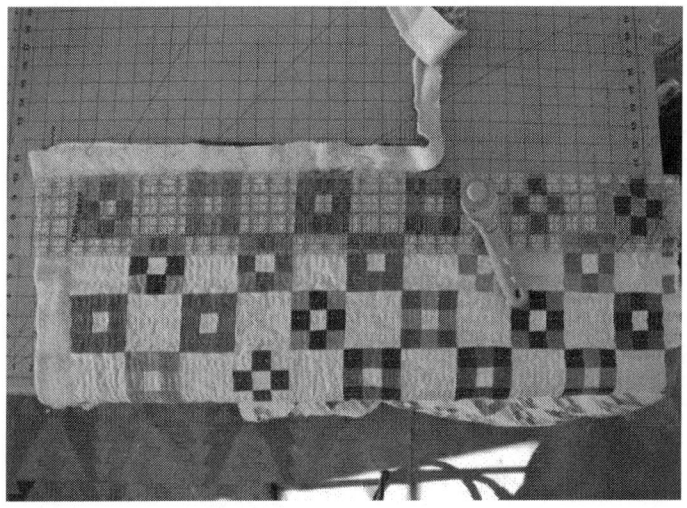

Step 2

Spare the Strips of Binding.

It is one of my favorite things to cut my pieces selvedge to selvedge, even though the more conventional method is to cut them on the bias.

Fold your binding cloth in half lengthwise now, making sure to line up the selvedges.

Note

Your quilt's perimeter and the length of each strip will determine the appropriate number of strips to use for your project, but the total number of strips needed may vary. To find out this information, you must first measure the entire perimeter of your quilt and then add about 20 inches to that number. Due to the fact that the perimeter of my quilt is 238 inches plus 20 more inches, this indicates that I will need binding strips that measure 258 inches. The width of my binding cloth is 52 inches, and the width of my binding fabric is also 52 inches. Divide the total perimeter of the quilt, which includes the additional 20 inches, by the width of the fabric used for the binding. According to what I can tell, dividing 258 inches by 52 inches results in the number 5, which tells me that I need to cut five binding strips.

Reduce the width of the binding strips so that they measure 2.75 inches. For double fold binding, I go with a width of this measurement.

Step 3

The next thing you need to do is join your individual binding strips together so that they form a single continuous strip. To begin, lay out two strips of fabric so that their right sides are facing each other and they are perpendicular to one another.

Step 4

Grab a marking pen (ideally a pencil) and a ruler. Begin at the bottom left corner's edge intersection and make your way up to the top right corner's edge intersection. Draw a diagonal line across using the marking pen.

Make an effort to be precise so that the binding tape you're using will have an even gap between each piece. As can be seen in the illustration that follows, the marking pen is placed precisely in the depression that is created when the two corners are brought together.

Now line up all of the pieces along the marked line, and stitch in a straight line along the line that has been marked.

It is recommended that seams be cut to a quarter of an inch (1/4) ") allowance

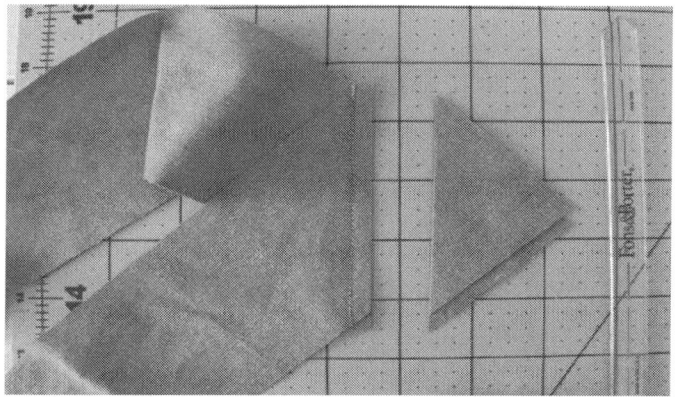

Step 5

1. Open up the seam and repeat the steps in the previous section until all of your binding strips have been joined into a single continuous strip using stitches.

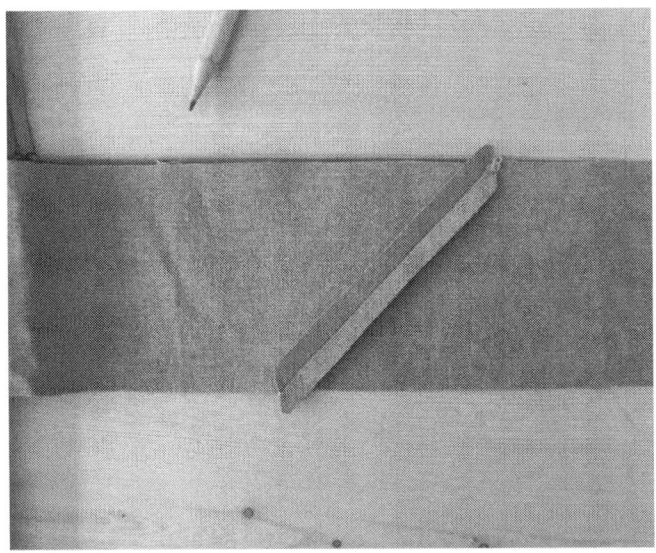

2. Folding the long piece of fabric in half lengthwise with the wrong sides

of the fabric facing each other and ironing the entire length of the binding with the wrong sides of the fabric facing each other are the steps that need to be taken with the long piece of fabric.

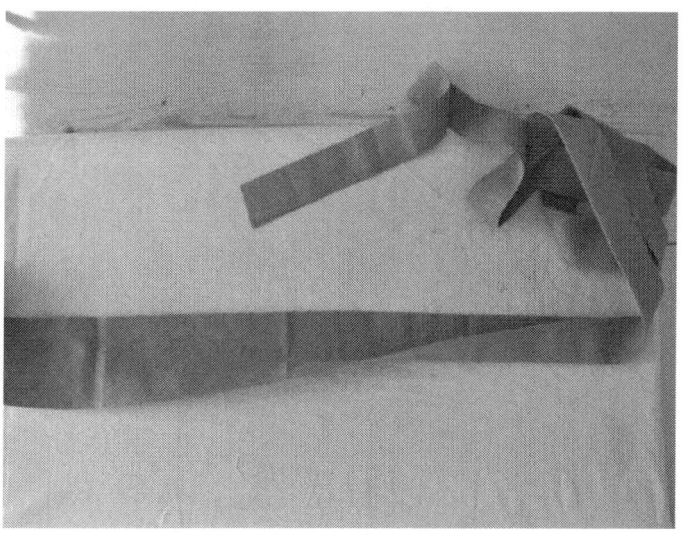

3. You should now have a strip of binding that is folded lengthwise, with the right sides showing, and the seams

should be on the inside of the folded binding piece.

Step 6

Stitch the binding along one of the edges of the quilt, beginning in the middle of one of the sides of your quilt. Return the binding to its original position, folding it in so that its raw corners align with the quilt's corners.

To begin, pin the binding to the top of the quilt, making sure that all of the unfinished edges are aligned properly. Leave approximately 10 inches of additional binding strip to hang loosely without being pinned. You will need to continue pinning the strip to the top of the quilt until you reach the end or corner of the quilt.

Step 7

Make a mark or stick a pin 1/4 of the way in "prior to the corner of the quilt. When you are sewing the binding onto the top of the quilt, use this mark or pin to designate the point at which you will stop stitching and remove the needle from the fabric.

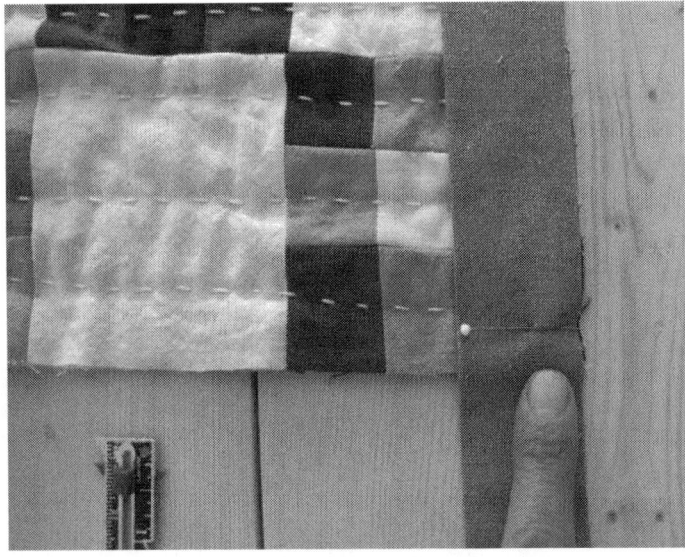

Step 8

1. Sewing the binding onto the top of the quilt with a seam that is 1/4 inches wide will secure it. Start in the middle of the quilt, leaving an additional 10 inches of binding unsewn, and making sure that the raw edges of the binding and the raw edges of the quilt are aligned.

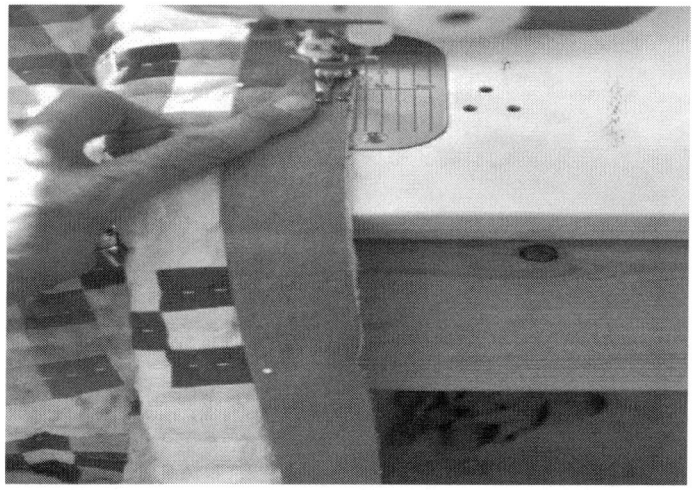

2. Stop stitching at the marked spot, which is 1/4 inch before the corner edge of the quilt.

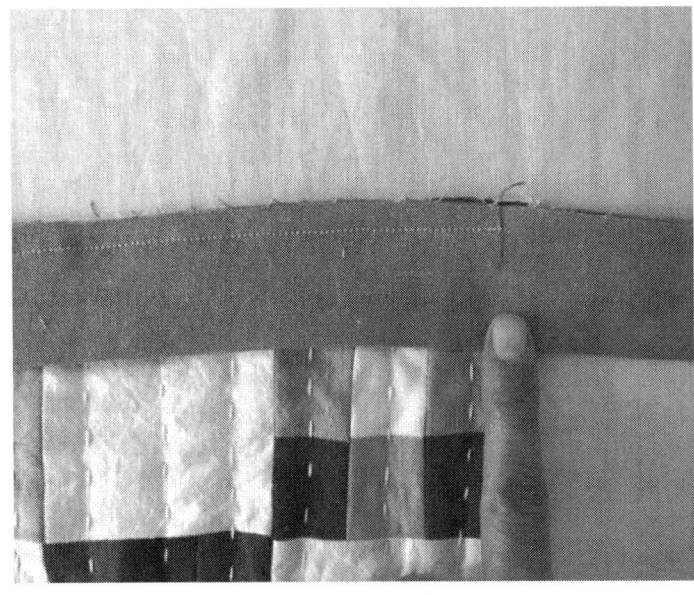

Step 9

1. Fold the binding strip in half lengthwise and lightly press with your

fingers or an iron to create a lovely mitered corner.

2. After that, fold the binding strip over itself in a direction that is perpendicular to the seam you just created. Press the binding while ensuring that the raw edge of the

binding is aligned with the raw edge of the quilt.

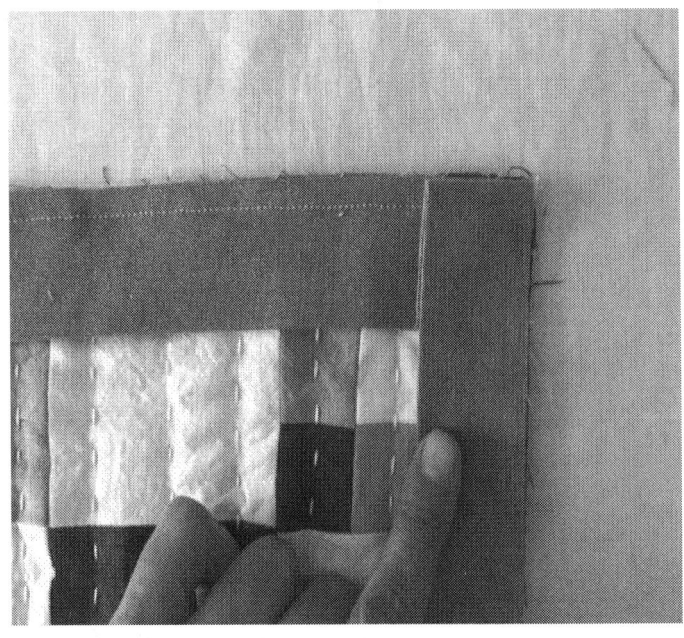

Step 10

Pinning the binding to the quilt's border should be done in the same manner as it was done previously. As you did in the previous step, begin stitching the binding down at the furthest edge and stop about 1/4 inch before reaching the edge or corner.

Step 11

You are going to continue stitching on your binding and mitering your corners in this manner until you get to the point where you started.

Give yourself some wiggle room for the next step by leaving at least a five to ten centimeter gap between where you start and where you finish. For the time being, the binding should look like the image shown below.

Step 12

1. Align the top raw edge of the additional binding strip on the left with the top raw edge of the quilt. Open out the additional binding strip.

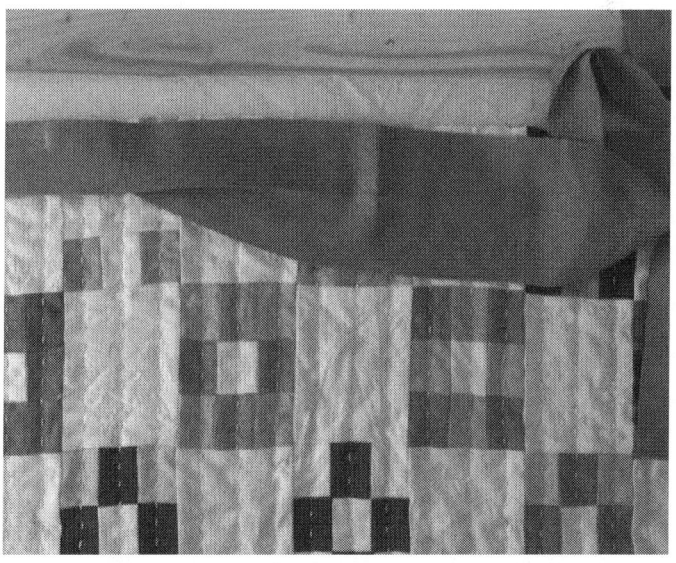

2. Open the binding piece on the right in essentially the same way as you did the piece on the left, fold it under and

up to make a 45-degree angle, and place it on top of the binding piece on the left, making sure to keep the top raw binding edge even with the quilt as shown in the image below. Put together the quilt so that the raw edges of the binding fabric are even with the edges of the quilt and that there are no puckers. We are currently attaching the binding to the quilt; however, we do not want it to be either too loose or too tight; rather, it should fit in a way that is natural against the edge of the quilt.

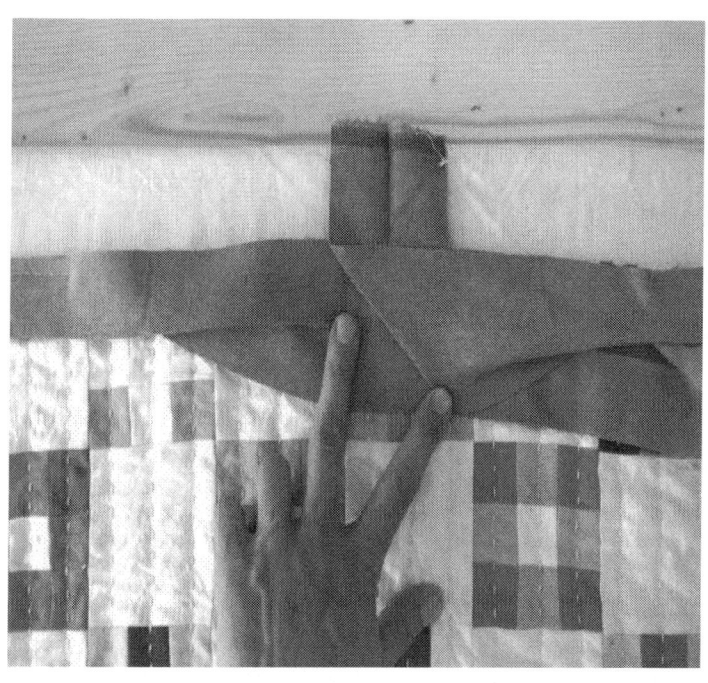

Step 13

Using your pencil, draw a line that corresponds to the 45-degree angle fold that is located on the bottom binding.

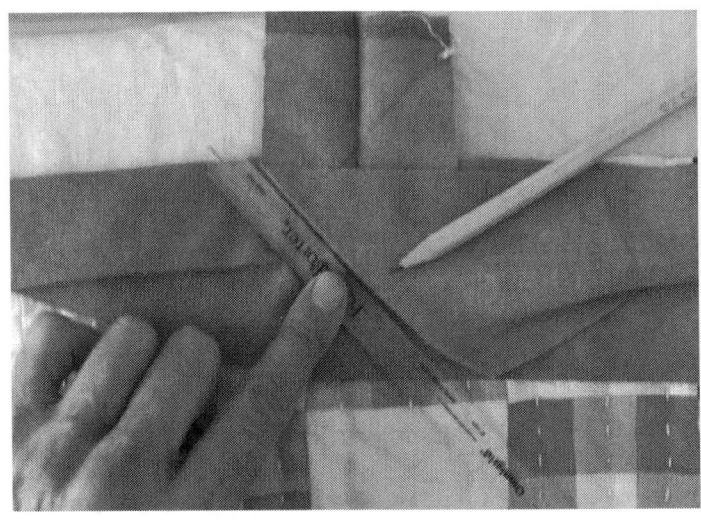

You can see the line I drew on the bottom binding in the following picture.

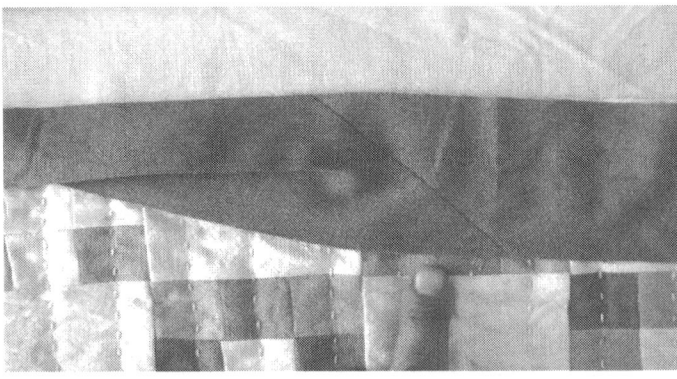

Step 14

1. Now, open up the right side binding piece, and along the crease, pin it together so that it stays in place. Put the crease of the fold in a straight position on top of the line. Transfer it with care to the sewing machine, and stitch along the folded crease, beginning and ending in the valley where the crease lines meet the corners, as was demonstrated in the previous step of the instructions.

2. The image that follows illustrates how it will appear once the sewing process has been finished. It is important that you pay attention to the excess fabric on both of the binding strips. After that, the binding will be trimmed, but before you do that, you should open it out and make sure that

it fits the quilt in the appropriate manner.

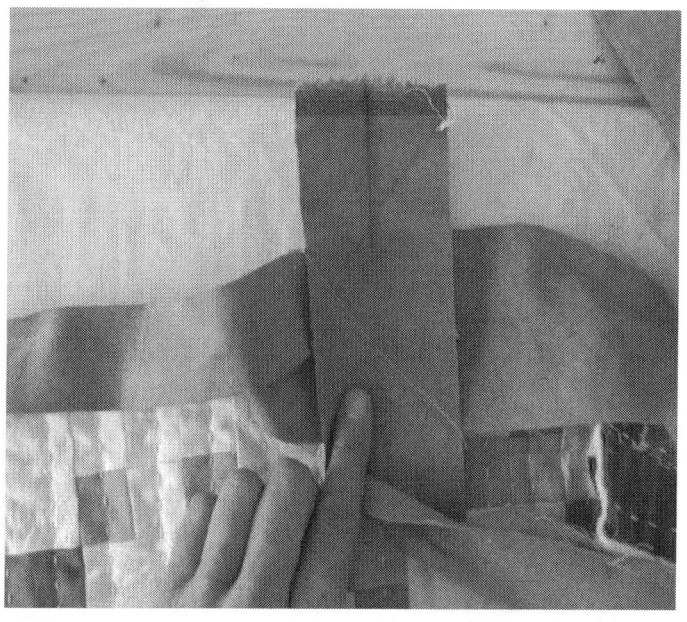

Step 15

Using either scissors or a rotary cutter in conjunction with a quarter-inch ruler, cut the seam to a length of 1/4 inch if the binding is the appropriate size for the quilt. After the seam has been trimmed, the opening should be pushed open. If the binding does not fit the quilt correctly, you will need to take the seam apart and try to fit the binding again.

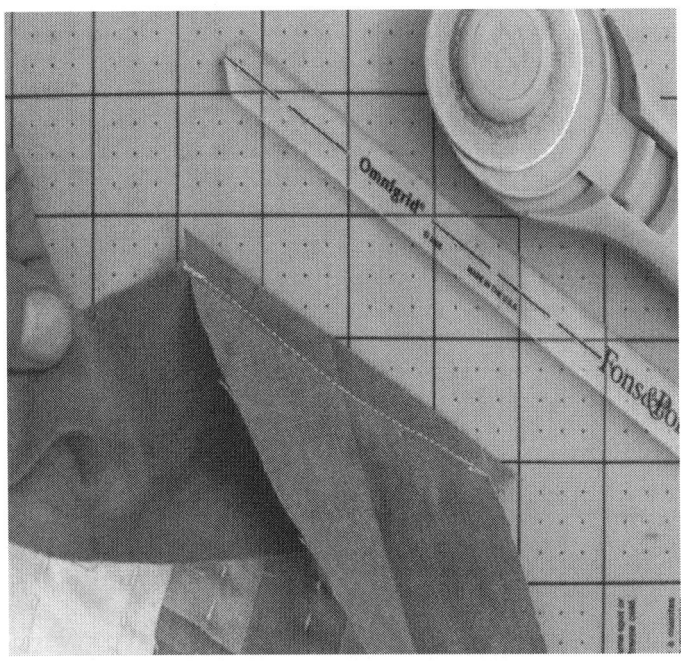

Step 16

The binding should be folded back along the initial fold, and then the two raw edges of the binding should be aligned with the raw edge of the quilt. Along the edge of the quilt's raw edge, the binding should have a relatively snug fit; it shouldn't be either too loose or too tight.

It is very clear where I began and ended stitching the binding to the edge of the quilt. Additionally, the diagonal seam that I used to ensure that the binding encircled the quilt in a manner that was secure is also very visible.

Transfer the quilt to the sewing machine while ensuring that the raw edge of the binding and the quilt are aligned with one another. Using a seam allowance of 1/4 inch, sew the remaining portion of the binding to the quilt. You might have to stretch the binding a little bit to get it to fit the quilt, but once you do that, it should fit perfectly and not pucker at all.

Step 17

Before you start ironing the quilt, turn it over on the ironing board so that the front is facing up. The back should be facing down. By folding the binding over from front to back, you can conceal the unfinished edge of the quilt. Pull it over just enough to hide the 1/4-inch seam that was created when sewing the binding to the front of the quilt. The seam was created when the binding was sewed to the front of the quilt. Maintain pressure and secure the binding with pins as you move forward.

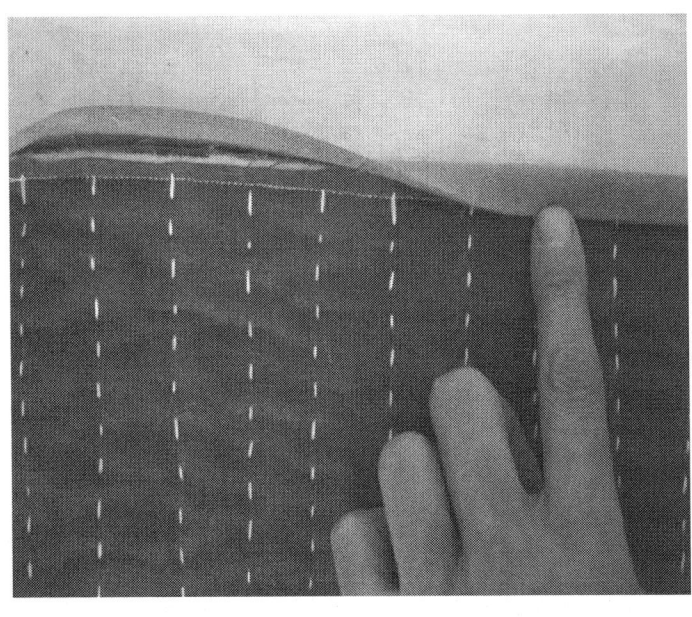

Step 18

I will use pictures to illustrate the mitered corners (just fold and pin, continue until the entire perimeter and mitering the corners is completed as see in the images beneath).

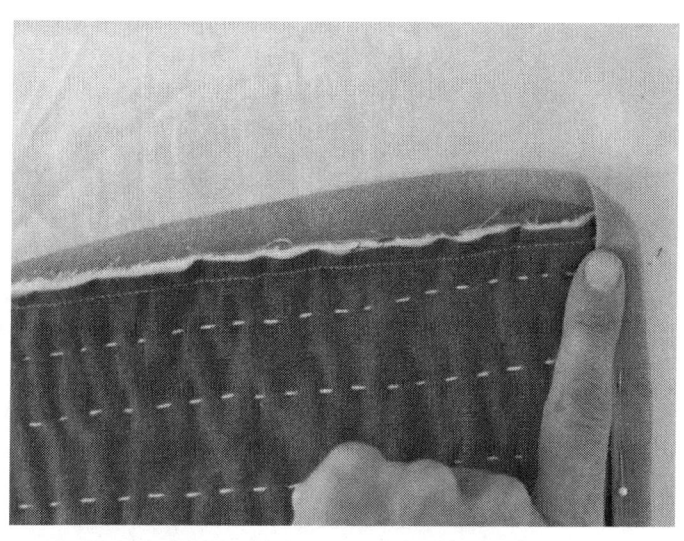
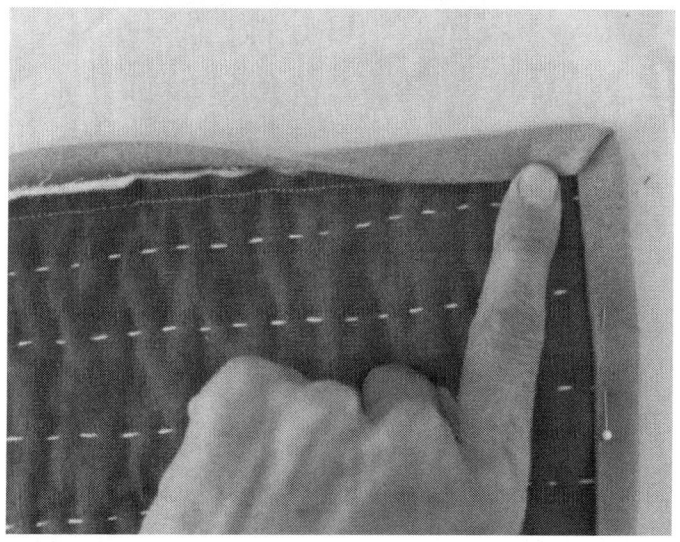

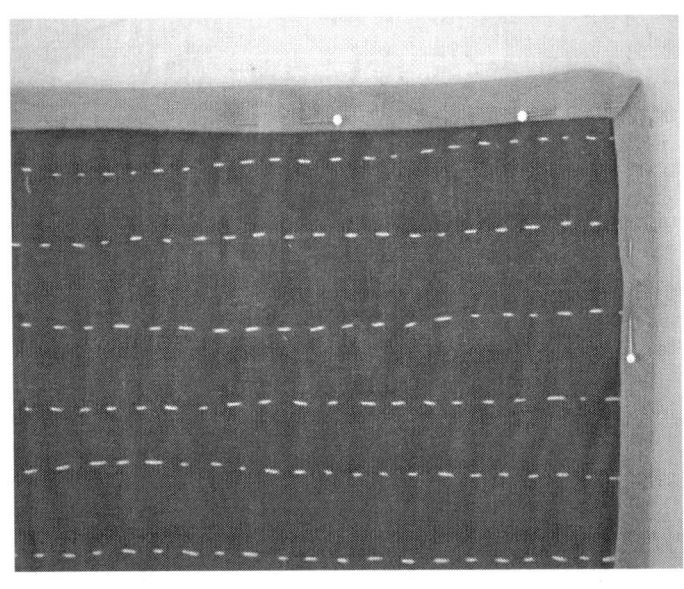

Step 19

It is time to hand stitch the binding in place after it has been mitered properly, pressed, and pinned along the entire perimeter. After this, it is time to press the binding. There are a few different approaches to using stitching to secure the binding. In this particular instance, I am not concerned with the accuracy of the stitches; however, you should check to make sure that your stitches do not pass through the quilt to the other side and the stitches should only be visible from the back. Make use of a sturdy thread that is a combination of cotton and silk and that, to some extent, complements the binding.

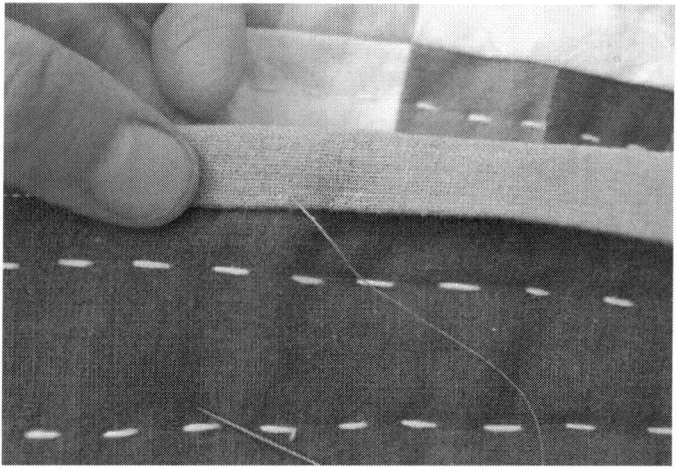

Step 20

The bottom stitches are visible, and this brings the whole thing together.

Top QAYG Tips

1. If you have access to fusible batting, use it whenever possible; doing so can assist reduce the amount of shifting that occurs while you stitch or quilt. In the event that the top is going to be sewn together, you should

fuse the batting to the backing of the cloth.

2. Make sure that both the backing and the batting are cut slightly larger than the top. After you have completed sewing it together and quilting it, cut the block down to the exact dimensions that are required. Sometimes things move, and even if you measure everything carefully and cut everything down to size before you begin, you may find that your parts are still somewhat smaller than they should be due of the change. You can save yourself some difficulty by beginning with a larger size and then trimming it down.

3. For the backdrop cloth, you might want to try choosing a busy print. Where the individual blocks are pieced together, there will be seams visible on the reverse of the finished product. Before you get started, it's a good idea to test out a few different fabrics with different patterns.

4. If a layer that you are sewing is significantly lighter than the cloth that is going on top of it and you are able to see through it, place a second piece of white fabric or muslin underneath the piece that you are adding to cover it up.

I'm hoping that you've gained some knowledge about the quilt-as-you-go technique, and that this little tutorial has inspired you to get started on a new quilt-as-you-go project as soon as possible. Happy crafting!

Manufactured by Amazon.ca
Bolton, ON

35661839R00050